"Keep watching, and maybe we'll get to see his head go indoors."

"When I get old enough to get married how will I know which girl to vote for?"

FAMILY CIRCUS®

HE FOLLOWED ME HOME!

Bil Keane

FAWCETT GOLD MEDAL • NEW YORK

A Fawcett Gold Medal Book
Published by Ballantine Books
Copyright © 1982 by Cowles Syndicate, Inc.
Copyright © 1987 by Cowles Syndicate, Inc.

Library of Congress Catalog Card Number: 86-91373

ISBN 0-449-12425-8

Printed in Canada

First Edition: April 1987

10 9 8 7 6 5 4 3 2 1

"It's an evergreen tree. You never get to see its skeleton."

"You don't hafta be afraid of him unless you're a fly."

"Is one for you and the other for Dolly?"
"No. One's for me and the other's for my tummy."

"Billy is learning to read. I like to help Billy. I listened to him read. Did you see me listen to Billy?"

"I couldn't eat any more right now, Mrs. Henry.
Can I have it in a doggy bag?"

"Uncles don't have wives. They have aunts."

"Could you leave out the kissing part?"

"Shall I let the tide out?"

"Your room always smells like summer."

"Claire's havin' a birthday party and she wants
a doll stroller, a monkey swing
or a mini-kitchen!"

"Mommy, if I ever get tattooed, where would you like to be on me?"

"Hide my meatballs under the spaghetti and see
if I can find them."

"PJ doesn't know how to rinse with fluoride. He
SWALLOWED it!"

"I didn't know you guys were goin' to a
MASQUERADE party, Mommy!"

"I must be growing real big. This drum won't hold me any more."

"I finished cleaning up my room, Mommy. Now what'll I do?"

"I rubbed every lamp in the house and nothing happened."

"I borrowed them for my robot."

"Hold it, Mommy! You've got 12 things here!"

"If the 'conomy doesn't get better I think Daddy might have to let a couple of us go."

"Mommy when you get old, how many grand-
children are you going to have?"

"Why does Grandma get a question mark on her cake instead of a number?"

"Wind is air in a hurry."

"Our teacher doesn't know much. Whenever she wants to know something she asks us."

"Maybe he'll grow up to be a tennis player."

"Which shall we clean first, Mommy — the nooks or the crannies?"

"I can touch my toes real easily,
Daddy. Watch."

"We're not allowed in until Mommy's finished
watchin' 'General Hospital.'"

"Well, what's it like bein' there with kangaroos
hopping around and throwin'
boomerangs, and. . . ."

"PJ's eating the doggy candies! Can
I have some?"

"'. . .Jack fell down and broke his crown. . . .'"
"Was Jack a KING?"

"The painter's here and he brought us passes
for today at the zoo!"

"It's not a truck, Dolly. It's a space shuttle!"

"I got all A's. APRIL FOOL!"

"I can hardly wait till I'M a paperboy, can you, Mommy?"

"This is fun, Mommy. I'm glad you wrecked
the car."

"I like eating lunch at school better 'cause I can eat my dessert first."

"I'm famous, Mommy! The teacher hung my
drawing on the wall!"

"When a commercial comes on could you change the sheets on my bed?"

"If we didn't have rain there wouldn't be any grass or flowers or mud."

"She's pushing back her cubicle."

"The lady justs wants to look at the price, Jeffy. She won't eat it."

"I don't think the Easter Bunny hid any up there, Billy."

"Grandma says the Easter Bunny left us each a basket at her house!"

"Why don't you just read the directions?"

"The boys are out with their dad and Dolly is having lunch."

"Well, can YOU come out and play?"

"Are we out of 'lectricity?"

"Where do mistakes go when you rub them out?"

"Draw me a bunny rabbit, Daddy."

"Wow! You mean you get to play video games
all day, Daddy?"

"I'm just practicin' to be like Milton Caniff!"

"Did you say 'browff'?"

"Yeah, my mom makes me carry one, too."

"Could you buy junk food when you were little, Grandma, or was it just homemade?"

"Mommy! It's raining popcorn!"

"WE should be called the waiters 'cause we do
all the waiting."

"We had to go to five different back yards to
find all these dandelions."

"I wish you'd have named me Al. Al Erb
already can spell his name and I'll
NEVER learn to spell Dolly."

"That money is for a
rainy day."

"Can I spend my money
now?"

"No, I don't think they knew her. This was long
before Miss Piggy was even born."

"Can I have a glass of water, Mommy? Our puddle is dryin' out."

"MAYDAY! MAYDAY!"

"Which music are you putting on -- exercising,
working, reading or dancing?"

"I can't remember, Mommy. Which little piggy was which?"

"Is this cereal new and improved or just the old kind?"

"PJ's finished his bottle!"

"Jeffy and I don't look ANYTHING alike so why do the neighbors keep mixin' up our names?"

"I made you toast and jelly for breakfast but I ate it."

"Dandelions are my favorite flowers. We can
pick them without getting in trouble."

"Would you talk us a book, Grandma?"

"I wish summer would wait until school's over."

"I only wore this shirt once. Do I hafta put it in the hamper?"

"Billy brought home a bad port re-card!"

"This is Armed Forces Day. Don't we get
chocolate soldiers?"

"He'll eat it if you pretend it's mud."

"Curds and whey . . . blackbird pies . . . boy!
They eat some weird stuff in that book!"

"We hafta be quiet while Mommy watches today's episoap."

"Oh yeah? What kind of flowers do ya want
on your grave?"

"That garage door sounds like thunder."

"Why are you burying that hole?"

"The hose lost its nostril."

"You guys hafta cut out the noise. Grandma said there's always a quiet before a storm."

"That's daddy when he was our brother."

"What's wrong with this compass, Daddy? The needle keeps pointing in the same direction all the time!"

"When me and PJ are old enough to go to school who's gonna stay home and take care of you?"

"It's broccoli."   "Check, please!"

"I want you back on earth before dark."

"Could we move to Wickenburg? Their team needs a pitcher."

"Mommy isn't playing, Daddy. She's looking for one of her serving spoons."

"Mommy, how do seedless grapes get baby grapes?"

"I'm getting real big, Grandma. I go all the
way from the floor up to here."

"You better not let Mommy catch you sitting here on the curve."

"You better write that letter to Grandma nice
and slow 'cause she doesn't read very fast!"

"All right, — WHOM do you think you're talking to?"

"Faster, Mommy! Faster!"

"We had to clean out our desks and the lost and found and the. . . ."

"No, no, Daddy! Don't forget what Sunday is!"

"Kneel down, Daddy. I can't hit the bat when it's that high."

"He's not coming unravelled, Dolly. He's
spinning a web."

"This grass is wet. It must've dewed last night."

"I didn't wanna get you mad, so I left them in the garage."

"The birds are DRINKING their bath water!"

"What do you shoot at those targets with,
Grandma?"

"I'll play cards with you, Daddy, but you keep
score — I don't know my numbers."

"Put those peas back on your plate, Pac-Man."

"Know why I like this ball? It never rolls under things."

"Look! These dandelions have turned into little pompons!"

"Now that I stopped sucking my thumb I only
have a couple more things to
learn to be a teen-ager!"

"I'd like to know what happened to all the dental floss."

"We went for a ride out where they keep all the scenery."

"Better not take the last one, Mommy, or you'll
be an old maid."

"This pot isn't any good. It has a hole in it."

"All our quarters were captured by the space people."

"I like them better on TV 'cause you can turn
the sound down."

"We're gonna have a park in our yard!"

"Billy! Don't wipe your face on your . . .   . . . sleeve!"

"We're gonna make a waterfall!"

"Well, Billy uses badder English than me."

"The balls kept tryin' to get into other people's games."

"Hey! I've got fingernails on my feet, too!"

"Do you think butterflies are the little children of angels?"

You can have lots more fun
with
BIL KEANE and
THE FAMILY CIRCUS